Stock Market Investing

Everything You Should Know About Stock Market Investing From Beginner To Advanced

Table of Contents

INTRODUCTION 5
CHAPTER 1 6
   WHAT IS THE STOCK MARKET? 6
   WHY DOES THE STOCK MARKET EXIST? 7
   HOW WAS THE STOCK MARKET FORMED? 8
   HOW DID IT DEVELOP TO WHAT IT IS TODAY? 10
   WHAT CAN THE STOCK MARKET DO FOR YOU? 11
   CAN YOU INVEST IN IT AS A SIDE JOB? 12

CHAPTER 2 – STARTING YOUR INVESTMENT CAREER 13
   WHAT DO YOU NEED? 13
   DISCOVER YOUR PERSONAL RISK TOLERANCE 16

CHAPTER 3 – SET YOUR PERSONAL FINANCE PRINCIPLES 17
   COVER YOUR BASIC NEEDS 17
   PAY OFF YOUR DEBTS..18
   CREATE AN EMERGENCY FUND 19
   BE SMART WITH YOUR FINANCIAL GOALS 20

CHAPTER 4 – SETTING YOUR FINANCIAL GOAL 22
   STEP 1: IDENTIFYING FUTURE GOALS AND EXPENSES......22
   STEP 2: SETTING A TARGET AMOUNT 23
   STEP 3: PLANNING THE SAVING TIMELINE....................24
   STEP 4: ASSESS THE AMOUNT OF GROWTH YOU NEED TO REACH YOUR GOALS 24
   STEP 5: PRACTICE WITH PAPER TRADING 25
   STEP 6: GET STARTED...26

CHAPTER 5 – CREATING YOUR CIRCLE OF COMPETENCE 27
   PICKING A SECTOR TO FOCUS ON 28

BECOMING A MASTER OF THE INDUSTRY 30
EXPLORING SPECIFIC COMPANIES 30
BEGINNING YOUR FUNDAMENTAL ANALYSIS 31
LEARNING TO READ FINANCIAL REPORTS 35

CHAPTER 6 – TIME YOUR ENTRY TO THE MARKET ..46

WHEN SHOULD YOU START BUYING? 46
READING CHARTS 48
THE REGULAR CANDLESTICK PLOT 49
HEIKIN-ASHI PLOT 50
CREATING TREND LINES 51
PICKING A STARTING POINT 53
SUPPORT AND RESISTANCE LINES 54
USING TREND LINES TO TIME YOUR ENTRY 55
USING MOVING AVERAGES AS BUYING SIGNALS 56
OTHER ADVANCED BUY INDICATORS 57

CHAPTER 7 – LEARNING ABOUT BUY AND SELL ORDERS 58

BASIC PARTS OF A BUYING ORDER 59
BUY LIMIT ORDERS 62
CREATING A SELL ORDER 65
STRATEGIES FOR PLACING ORDERS 66

CHAPTER 8 – DIVERSIFYING YOUR ASSET DISTRIBUTION 69

CHAPTER 9 – PLANNING AN EXIT STRATEGY 74

BASING YOUR EXIT STRATEGY ON THE PRICE 74
USING FUNDAMENTALS TO GUIDE YOUR EXIT 75
BASING YOUR DECISION ON YOUR FINANCIAL GOALS 75
USING TECHNICAL ANALYSIS TO SIGNAL YOUR EXIT 76

CHAPTER 10 – BE AWARE OF THE CYCLES IN THE MARKET 79

THE JANUARY EFFECT 80
UNITED STATES PRESIDENTIAL ELECTION CYCLE 81
THE RAY DALIO MODEL OF DEBT CYCLES 82

CHAPTER 11 – COMMON INVESTING MISTAKES BY BEGINNERS 90

CHAPTER 12 – IMPORTANT BEGINNER TIPS 95
- RECORD ALL YOUR ACTIONS 95
- KEEP ON GOING EVEN IN THE FACE OF LOSSES 96
- BE WARY WHEN EVERYONE IS EXCITED 97
- AVOID INVESTING WITH BORROWED MONEY 99
- CREATE A STOCK BUILDING CIRCLE OF FRIENDS 100
- LEARN TO HEDGE YOUR POSITION 101
- DON'T FEEL BAD FOR EXITING EARLY 102

CONCLUSION 103

Introduction

The world of investing is an intimidating but rewarding one. Since the turn of the century, we have seen two massive economic crashes, countless people losing their savings and retirements, multiple Ponzi schemes, and stories of people who lost everything in the stock market.

This does not stop people however, from returning to the market and investing. It seems that most have forgotten the events of 2008. Most people are taking their chances again in the market, hoping to earn a quick buck.

How do you come out on top as an investor in the midst of all this uncertainty and chaos?

This book will guide you on how you can earn money consistently in the stock market. Using the information you will gain from it, you will be able to create a portfolio filled with high value stocks. In addition, you will learn how to start investing by working on your personal finance habits and your financial goals.

Further it will provide you with the information on how you can set financial goals and choose stocks that will help you reach such goals. We also go into the details of making a stock transaction.

Most importantly, this book will provide you with the best practices of investing. It will help you to understand when to buy and when to sell through the use of fundamental analysis, technical analysis, proper diversification and awareness of stock market economic cycles.

Chapter 1 – Stock Market Basics

"An investment in knowledge pays the best interest."

~Benjamin Franklin

The majority of the public do not understand what the stock market is. We've seen movies about it, but most of them were made simpler for us regular folks to understand. You cannot start investing not knowing what company stocks are and what their purpose is.

The first rule in any kind of investing is to "invest in what you know". In this chapter, we will discuss what the stock market really is and why every free market society has one.

What is the stock market?

The stock market is the overall platform in which people and organizations buy and sell stocks. Most developed country has at least one stock exchange. The stock exchange is a private company that manages and maintains the stock market. They provide the technology and the people needed to allow transactions to happen in the market. Put simply, the stock market is where you buy and sell stocks.

You may be asking, what exactly are stocks?

Stocks (also called equities or shares) are units that represent a person's claim to a company's assets and earnings. Companies sell these units to raise funds. The people who buy them are called stockholders (or shareholders). By selling stocks, companies give these investors a claim for their assets and future earnings.

Why does the stock market exist?

The stock market is an important part of the economy. To understand why it is necessary, you could put yourself in the shoes of the different stakeholders in the market.

First, you have the companies selling the stocks. They need the stock market to raise funds. The funds that they raise can be used for a number of growth-oriented business activities. For instance, the money could be used to develop more production assets. Increased production could lead to higher profits and this could increase the overall value of the company. The stock market could allow these companies to grow at a rate that may not be possible otherwise.

Next, we have the policy makers and the government in general. People in the government use the stock market and other investment markets as a litmus test for the economy. When consumers are in the mood for buying stocks and other securities, this may be an indicator that many people have money to spare. This is a good sign for the government because it shows that people have more money than they need for their basic needs. The activities in the stock market is also one of the factors that policy makers use when deciding to implement new financial policies.

Policies such as printing new money and changing the Federal Interest Rate are heavily dependent on the activities of investors in the market.

Lastly, we have the investors. When you start investing your money, you become a part of this group. The stock market allows you and other regular people to invest in the companies that you are familiar with. In the process, you aid the growth of the economy and if done right, you may be able to grow your money.

How was the stock market formed?

The stock market was not formed in a day. No one person invented it. Instead, it was formed over the centuries of people practicing mercantilism. The first stock market could be credited to the Dutch in the 1600s. While they are the first in recorded history to actually facilitate the sale of company stocks, the way may have been paved by the Italians who began selling other types securities as early as the 13th century.

At around this time, the governments of Venice, Pisa, Verona, Florence and many other city states worked with banks to sell government bonds to raise government funds. This was followed by the actual selling of company shares. However, there is no record stating that there is a formal meeting place for the sales of these shares. The stock certificates were bought and sold in person or through banks. They were also bought and sold among people who knew each other and were not generally available to the public.

It wasn't until the 1600s that the first marketplace for selling these unique types of securities first emerged. It was at this time that the Dutch East India Company offered its company stocks to the public. Their company stocks were sold in the Amsterdam Exchange.

While today's trading experience uses computers and other digital tools, in the past, it was all done through ledgers and certificates. The stockholders of a company were written in a ledger. They are also given stock certificates as a receipt that they can show as proof that they are indeed stock holders.

In the United States, the earliest record of an organized exchange can be traced to the Buttonwood Agreement in the late 1700s. This agreement set the stage for the creation of the New York Stock Exchange (NYSE). The NYSE is the largest stock exchange in the world today. However, it started out as a small exchange that only traded government bonds. The first company stocks to be traded in the exchange were those of banks.

As the market grew, so did the exchange that managed it. In the past, the trades were done in tables in the streets and in coffee shops around New York. The exchange transferred its location multiple times before it settled in the now-iconic 11 Wall Street, Lower Manhattan, New York City, New York.

How did it develop to what it is today?

The evolution of Wall Street is closely connected with the development of communication technology. In the early days, only people around New York knew about the stock market and only the rich had the resources and the manpower to keep track of price changes in the market. People from other parts of the United States could not participate in the market unless they sent a representative to the exchange.

Everything changed with the development of the telegraph machine. With the help of this tool, people from far and wide were able to learn the stock prices sooner. This allowed investors from other parts of the country to participate in the market.

The development of other communication tools further increased access to the market. As the telephone became more common, it became one of the primary ways to connect with the market. Investors often talked with their brokers through the phone. They called their brokers to give transactional instructions.

The stock market was also one of the earliest industries to make use of the internet as a practical business tool. It all started when the National Association of Securities Dealers Automated Quotations (NASDAQ) provided digitalized priced quotes. This made it easier for investors and other market participants to keep track of market activities.

With the internet becoming more popular in the 90s, it was just a matter of time before it was used as a trading tool. In 1994, the company K. Aufhauser & Company, Inc. offered the first online trading platform.

Today, modern brokerages allow investors to do their own trades. They no longer needed to connect with a broker. Instead, investors can now place orders or stop existing orders through their online browser-based accounts.

Now that you have an idea about the stock market and your role in it, let's talk about what you need to get started.

What can the stock market do for you?

As you may already know, the stock market is one of the best ways to make money. There are two general ways that you can use to make your money in the stock market grow. First, you can increase the value of your money by earning dividends. Dividends are cash rewards that the company pays its investors. The dividends usually come from excess company profits and the amount that you will get depends on the number of shares that you own of a particular company.

The second way to earn using the stock market is through buying and selling stocks. This method is called capital appreciation. In this method, you buy the stocks and sell them later on when the price of the stocks increase. This is how most participants in the stock market make money.

Can you invest in it as a side job?

Investing directly in the stock market requires a certain degree of commitment. You can successfully invest by allocating only 5-8 hours a day to it. You will spend most of this time exploring the options in the stock market, studying charts and designing your trading approaches and strategies.

While you can do most of these things when the market is closed, it's best to focus on the market when it is open. You can integrate the activities of checking the events in the market and checking the performance of your current investing positions to your daily work activities.

To answer the question above, you can do it as a side job, but make sure that you do due diligence when investing. Take the time to study the companies you are looking to invest on.

You may also need to adjust your personal strategy based on the amount of time that you can spend on the market. If you have more time to spend, you can take active trading decisions. This is a type of trading where in you buy and sell your positions after a few days or weeks. You cannot take the same types of positions when you cannot keep your eyes on the market.

If you can only spend a small amount of time per week on the stock market on the other hand, it's best to choose long term positions when investing. Long term positions focus on trades that take months or even years to compete.

Chapter 2 – Starting your Investment Career

"The individual investor should act consistently as an investor and not as a speculator."

~Ben Graham

It is now easier than ever to trade in the stock market. The internet has significantly decreased the barrier to entry to the market. In the past, people needed to have a large investment capital to start investing in the stock market. Brokers generally did not accept small volume trades because it was not worth their while. Nowadays, you can start investing for a little as $100 because you no longer need to talk to brokers to start trading.

The increased access to the market however, has also increased the percentage of people losing money. Investors are most prone to mistakes when they are just starting out. Because this, it's best to learn everything you can about the process of buying and selling before you actually start investing.

Let's start with the things you need to start investing:

What Do You Need?

- Initial Capital

To start investing, you will need an investment capital. This is the money you will use to buy stocks. To become successful in your investing career, you need to learn to manage your money. In particular, you need to be able to separate your investment money from the rest of your money. The initial capital is the fund that you will use solely for investing. It needs to be separate from other types of funds from your life such as the money that you use for your everyday needs.

- Find an Honest and Fair Broker

The brokerage firm is the company that will facilitate your stock trades for you. In today's market, most brokers no longer provide investing advice. They only facilitate the transactions that you need to do by providing you with the technological tools that you will need. By stripping their services, brokers are able to provide their services to the public with minimal fees.

When looking for a brokerage firm, you want one that has a good reputation of being secure. You also want to ensure that their interface is easy to use. This is particularly important for beginners. Most beginners lose money because they do not understand the interface of the trading tool that they are using.

Aside from the tools and the data they provide, you also want to look into the fees of the brokerage firm. Compare their fees to the other brokers in the market. You want to sign up with a brokerage firm that takes the least amount of fees. These firms charge you for each transaction. That means that you will need to pay them every time you buy or sell stocks.

It's good practice to keep track of the amount of money that you pay on fees. This will allow you to adjust your practices in investing to avoid racking up larger fees.

- Investing Goal

You also need to have an investing goal, even before you start with your first transaction. A goal gives you a target to aim for. It motivates you to do well in your trades. It also encourages you to stick the best practices of trading and to avoid practices that will increase the risk of losing money. Lastly, the investing goal will help guide you in your decision making process. If your goal's deadline is still far for instance, you could still take risks on high-risk/high-return stocks. However, as your goal's deadline draws nearer, it's best to stick to low-risk stocks to protect any profit that you have already gained. This is just one example of how you can use your goal as a guide in investing.

- Preferred Investment Strategy

Lastly, you will need to set your own investment strategy. An investment strategy is a set of actions that you plan to do in the market that will allow you to reach your investment goals. It may say what types of company stocks you will focus on or your conditions for entering a trade. We will discuss more on investment strategies later in the book.

Discover your Personal Risk Tolerance

Each person has a different reaction to risk, especially when there is money involved. Most people are not comfortable with taking risks. This is particularly common for people with a small amount of fund to use in investing. They are more reactive to the market.

On the other hand, there are people who are almost immune to risk. Losses do not affect their attitude towards an investment.

The degree in which you can tolerate risk will help you in the types of strategies that you will use in investing. Ideally, you could even use it as your basis for selecting the stocks that you will invest in.

Before you start investing, you could first take a risk tolerance assessment test to see your own reaction to risk. It takes a high level of risk tolerance to invest in the stock market because of the constant fluctuations in the prices of stocks. If you do not like risk at all, it is best that you stock to less risky investment tools like bonds and money market funds.

To learn about your personal risk tolerance, there are exams online that you can take. These exams are just a series of situational questions that aim to take your reaction to certain types of events. Be honest when answering the test to get an accurate assessment of your risk appetite.

You can start by taking the personal tolerance test in the website of University of Missouri Personal Financial Planning Program:

http://pfp.missouri.edu/research_IRTA.html

Chapter 3 – Set Your Personal Finance Principles

"The stock market is filled with individuals who know the price of everything, but the value of nothing."

~Phillip Fisher

It is not ideal to invest in the stock market if you are having money problems. You could try to sort out any financial issues you have before investing your money. In this chapter, we will talk about how you can manage your money so that you will not lose everything in case your investments go south. Let's start with your basic needs:

Cover your basic needs

Your basic needs are urgent. Investing your money should be the least of your problems if your family is having trouble putting food on the table.

To cover your basic needs, you first need get a job that pays enough to cover your needs and the needs of your dependents. A part of your income needs to go to the things that you need to pay off regularly such as your food budget, your mortgage/rent and your bills.

A key part to becoming a good investor is to be efficient in the way you use your money. Try to apply efficiency in the way you manage your money by letting go of recurring expenses that you do not need. If you are paying too much for your cellphone bills for instance, you can try to find a plan with a lower monthly cost. If you buy cooked food regularly for instance, you could try cooking your own food to see if you will be able to save money. These are just some simple changes you can apply to your life to start saving money.

The money you save will go to two important prerequisites of investing: debt payment and saving for your emergency fund.

Pay off your debts

Financial commitments that gain interest will eat away at your net worth unless you deal with them as soon as possible. The longer you keep your debts, the bigger they become. You need to deal with them before you can start investing.

If you have debts, it's best to take a percentage of your savings and allocate it to your debt payments. If you have borrowed money from different sources, choose to pay off the ones with the highest interest rate. These debts will grow faster than the rest so you need to deal with them while they are still small. Only start investing if you are free from debts.

Once you start paying off your debt, it's wise to avoid signing up for more debts. This means that you need to avoid buying anything that would require you to borrow money. If you need to borrow money to buy something, then you probably cannot afford it.

It's easier to accumulate debt when you have a credit card. Today, it's almost impossible not to use your credit card on daily purchases. To prevent your credit card spending from growing, make sure that you pay them off on time every month. You could do this by setting your bank to automatically deposit a payment to your credit card company.

Create an emergency fund

If you have no debts, you may put your savings on your emergency fund. The emergency fund is a sum of money that you set aside to be used only during emergency situations. This includes emergency purchases, hospitalization expenses, legal fees and other similar scenarios.

The emergency fund is important because it protects your other assets in times of emergencies. It will allow you to deal with misfortunes without the need to get a loan or to use your money in your investment portfolio.

As a rule of thumb, your emergency fund needs to be at least six times the size of your monthly expenses. Many people think that this amount is too big. However, it's better to have enough money in the bank in case your income suddenly stops. If you lose all your sources of income for example, you will have enough savings for six months to be able to find a job. By having an emergency fund, you will not be forced to take jobs that you do not want to take.

It is also important that you replenish your emergency fund when you do use it. By making sure that your emergency fund is always full, you will always be ready in case an emergency happens.

Be smart with your financial goals

Now that you have dealt with your debt and you have enough money for emergencies, it's time to talk about how investing can be used to make you reach your goals faster. There are two general types of financial goals, short term goals and long term goals.

Save for your short term goals

There are some types of goals that you will not be able to invest for. It's usually not a good idea to invest money that is meant for a short term goal. If an unforeseen event happens that will pull the value of your investment down, you will not have enough time to recover the money you've lost in the market.

It's best to save for these short term goals the traditional way. You could simply put these funds in bank accounts that have the highest interest rates. This way, they will still grow in the time when you are stashing them. Bank products like savings accounts and time deposits allow your money to gain interest without exposing it to market-related risks.

It's best to use this strategy for goals that are less than two years long. If you plan on using a specific savings fund within two years, do not put it in the stock market.

Invest for your long term goals

The stock market is better suited for investment goals that you can give yourself more than 2 years to meet. Ideally, you want to use it to boost the value of goal funds that will be used in 5-7 years.

With these types of goals, your money will be idle for a long time. While your money is idle, it's best to put your money to work by putting it in the stock market.

Investing for your long term goals also lessens the amount of pressure you feel when investing. You will not be pressured to buy stocks that promise great returns, because you still have time to take less risky routes towards your goal.

On the other hand, if you urgently need your money to grow, you are in danger of taking on more risk than necessary. You may be forced to invest in companies you know nothing about. You may also be tempted to keep your money in a position longer than you should.

Most importantly, if you are investing for long term goals, you have time to recover from mistakes. If you made the mistake of putting your entire portfolio in the market back in 2007, you may have lost 35-40% of its value. If you were investing for a short term goal at that time, there wouldn't have been enough time for you to recover your losses. If your financial goals are still far off, you may have time to recover some it by keeping your funds in the market for 3-5 years.

Chapter 4 – Setting your Financial Goal

"Financial peace isn't the acquisition of stuff. It's learning to live on less than you make, so you can give money back and have money to invest. You can't win until you do this."

~Dave Ramsey

After dealing with your debts and saving for an emergency fund, the next step is to plan what you will use your money for. Allocation of resources is one of the most basic problems that the study of economics tries to deal with. This problem exists because we have a limited amount of resources and an endless list of needs and wants.

The key to solving this problem on a personal level is to identify the needs and wants that you want to prioritize the most. You may do this by looking into the different options where you can spend your money on and identify the ones that you really want to work for. Let's start with the first step:

Step 1: Identifying Future Goals and Expenses

Setting a solid financial goal starts with your ideas. You may start by thinking of the things that you want to buy in the future. Most of us are already doing this. However, only a few actually do more than think about their dreams. Instead, most people only do wishful thinking and hope that one day they will have enough money to achieve their goals.

To start your own goal setting process, make a list of the things that you want to buy in the future. Some of the things that you may have in your list may be really important like buying a home or setting up a retirement fund. Others, like taking a big vacation or buying a sports car are not as important but they may make us happier.

After creating your list, put a number beside each item with the number 1 assigned to the most important goal. Here is a sample list that you can base your own on:

1. Create a Wedding Fund
2. Buy a home that's big enough for the family
3. Save for kids' college fund
4. Save for dream travel destination

Some goals have a predetermined deadline. If you have kids for example and you are saving for their college fund, the fund needs to be ready by the time they graduate from high school.

Step 2: Setting a Target Amount

When working for your financial goals, you need to deal with them one at a time. While we want to achieve all the goals in our list, we are more likely to accomplish goals faster when we focus our financial resources on the ones that are most important to us. When that particular goal is done, we could move on the next task on our list.

Step 3: Planning the Saving Timeline

Now that you have your financial goals set, pick the most important one and set the timeline for saving for that goal. By plotting the timeline, you will be able to know how long you have to save for the goal.

As we've discussed in the previous chapter, it's best to invest in the stock market only for your long term goals to lessen the risk. Pick a financial goal that is still a couple of years away from completion and set it as the target of your stock investing activities.

Step 4: Assess the amount of growth you need to reach your goals

The general idea behind investing is that you will need to make your savings grow so that you will reach your financial goals faster. You want to set the right expectations when it comes to the growth potential of your investments. Some of your trades will yield north of 15% while others will end up with losses. It is more realistic to expect a modest rate of return of 7% to 10% each year. Some beginners who make early mistakes in the stock market may experience even lower rates of return on their first few years of trading. While these rates of return may seem low, they are still better than many of the investment opportunities out there.

Knowing the average rate of return in the market, you will be able to make assumption on how long it will take for your funds to grow to reach your target amount. If you have $10,000 right now and you invest it and get an average of 8% rate of return per year, it will take you more than 9 years to reach a $20,000 target. You can increase the rate of reaching that target by adding more capital to your fund each month. You may also increase the rate of growth by taking high growth rate stocks in the beginning of the trading period.

To learn the relationship of the rate of return to the amount of time it takes you to reach your goal, use a compounding interest calculator. In this type of calculator, you will need to enter the capital amount, the number of years that you will be investing, and the annual rate of return you are expecting to get the final amount. Any additional income you earn in the market will be reinvested to it to create a compounding effect. This will help you reach your target amount faster.

Step 5: Practice with Paper Trading

If you find that the stock market is the best place to invest for your financial goals, you can increase your chances of success by practicing your trades. You can start practicing by doing trades on paper.

You can start a paper trade by taking a notebook and taking notes of the stocks that you want to invest in. You could then start by choosing one of these stocks and do a mock trade. In your mock trade, you pick the stock; you also identify your buying price and the volume of your purchase. Lastly, you set the conditions where in you will sell the stock. In the following days, months or years, you could then start to track the stock that you picked to assess the performance of your mock trade.

You could make the mock trade even more realistic by creating a budget that is similar to the budget that you will have when you actually start trading. This will prevent you from being reckless in your stock picks.

Mock trades like this allow you to practice with your trading strategies. If your mock trades often end up with losses, you may need to make changes in your trading strategy.

Paper trades also allow you to become more familiar with the market and the different events that are going on in the moment before you even participate in the market. It allows you to experience how it would be like to invest in the companies that you consider to be within your circle of competence.

The key to paper trading is to do it as many times as you can. This will allow you to know which indices, sectors and companies are most profitable.

Step 6: Get Started

Now that you know what you want to achieve and what you need to achieve it, start working on your financial goals. You can begin by saving for your investment capital. Ask your broker for the minimum amount that you will need to start investing. While you are saving, start studying the companies that you will buy with your initial investment amount. This will ensure that you will be ready to start investing when you have saved the minimum investing amount needed.

Chapter 5 – Creating your Circle of Competence

"Price is what you pay. Value is what you get."

~Warren Buffett

Each stock exchange in the US contains thousands of listed companies. It is impossible for you to examine each of these companies and create an informed decision on which companies to invest in.

Even the best investors in the world do not go through each of these companies. Instead, they focus on a group of companies that they have studied in detail for years. Warren Buffet call these companies the Circle of Competence.

To start your investing journey, you also want to create your own circle of competence. You can begin by picking a sector to start with.

Picking a Sector to Focus On

A sector is a segment of the stock market that offers similar sets of markets and generally caters to the needs of the same market. It is a general category of companies that share a similar nature of business. The financial sector for example, may include banks, investment companies and lending companies. They all generally do business related to money.

The US stock market is made of 11 sectors:

- Energy
- Materials
- Industrials
- Consumer Discretionary
- Consumer Staples
- Health Care
- Financials
- Information Technology
- Telecommunication Services
- Utilities
- Real Estate

These sectors can be subdivided further into subsectors. These subsectors further specify the nature of the business of the company.

When you are just starting out, you want to first study the sectors and subsectors that you are already familiar with. If you spend a lot of time reading about technology news for instance, you may already be familiar with many of the companies and the current events in the technology sector. You may even delve deeper in the Computer Manufacturing subsector. This is where you will see popular tech companies like Apple Inc. (AAPL), Dell Technologies Inc. (DVMT) and HP (HPE).

It will be faster and easier for you to learn about sectors that you are already familiar with and you are interested in. If you choose to learn about a sector that you are not familiar with, you may end up spending more time than necessary researching and reading about them. You may become stuck when you encounter industry jargons that are only known to those who are already in the industry.

If there is no one sector that you are already knowledgeable about, you could pick an industry that you are genuinely interested in. This way, learning will not be as hard because you enjoy reading about the industry.

You could also choose an industry where you participate as a consumer. If you spend a lot on clothes and apparels for instance, you could also choose to learn about the companies in the Clothing/Shoe/Accessory Stores subsector. This subsector is included in the Consumer Services sector and it includes some of the biggest clothing brands like Gap Inc. (GPS), Nike (NKE) and Nordstrom Inc. (JWN).

Becoming a Master of the Industry

After picking a sector to invest in, you want to spend at least a couple of hours a day learning about it. First, you want to know all the notable companies in the sector. Know which companies are competing against each other and what has been going on in the industry in the past six months.

By learning about the companies inside a sector of subsector, you should be able to know the products and services that they represent. It also helps to learn which companies are getting the dominant part of the market share in their respective industries.

If you are looking for value companies to invest in, you may also look into some of the big companies that aren't listed in the market yet. If an up and coming company is doing well in competing with the big and established companies, the newer companies may choose to become a listed company in the future. If there is such a company in your chosen sector, you may want to be a part of that initial public offering.

Exploring Specific Companies

Next, you want to look into specific companies in your chosen sectors and subsectors. You want to look into companies that have a good potential of growing in the future in accordance with your investment goals.

When exploring companies, you want to look deeper into their products and their core competencies. The core competencies refer to the qualities of a company that makes it stand out from its competitors. Apple Inc. for instance, stands out from their opponents in the industries in many ways. For instance, their brand has a cult following that is lacking among Android smartphone users. This means that their brand has a big number of loyal fans all over the world who will buy just about anything that they choose to sell.

Beginning your Fundamental Analysis

When you start to look into these things, you are beginning the process of fundamental analysis. Fundamental analysis refers to the careful scrutiny of the business of a company. In this kind of analysis, you try to learn everything you can about the business activities of a company. By doing fundamental analysis on a company, you try to learn its strengths and weaknesses compared to the companies that it is competing with. Here is some of the information that you would want to find out:

How is the company making money?

The goal of every listed company is to make money. This could come either from selling products or providing services to people, other businesses or to governments. For a company to succeed, it needs a solid product that the market loves to spend on. They also need a business model.

The business model is the plan on how the company will make money. It includes a combination of operational processes, revenue sources, customer base and marketing and financing.

If the business model is solid, it will allow the company to make money. However, not all business models are successful. Sometimes, the people who design the business model fail to take some important factors into consideration.

A retail store for instance seems like a simple business model. All a business needs to do is to start a store in a busy part of the city and to sell many products. However, sometimes entrepreneurs fail to consider factors like the competition that's already established in the market and the behavior of the consumers. When some important business factors are overlooked, there is a good chance that the business model will fail.

Because of this, you need to put a lot of time into studying the business model of the company that you are considering investing in.

How much is the company making?

Now that you know how a company makes money, the next step is to learn how much they are making.

First, you want to know the gross margin of the company with their products. The gross margin is the difference between the selling price of the product or service and the total cost of producing that product or providing the service. A strong company will have a high gross margin. The higher the gross margin of your product, the fewer products you need to sell to make a lot of profit.

This information is especially important when you are comparing competing companies. If two companies produce similar products, but one company can produce their products at half the price, then that company will have a better chance of success, with all other factors being equal.

Next, you want to learn three important finance related information, the gross revenue, the operational expenses and the net income. The gross revenue is the total sales revenue of the company. As you may already know, you want this number to be lower. Next, you want to subtract the operational expenses from company's revenue to get the net profit. A strong company keeps their operational expenses low so that their net profit will still be high.

In a competitive industry, some companies may opt to use their revenue to improve their business. When done properly, spending the revenue on the business may lead to the growth of the company. This usually reflects in an increase in the operational expenses. Investors don't really mind an increase in the operational expenses if it leads to higher revenue in future reports.

This does not always happen though. Sometimes the money earned is spent inefficiently. When this happens, the increased operational expenses do not bear any fruit. The market will not like this and it may lead to a decrease in the stock value.

Who are the people leading the company?

For a company to become successful, the people leading it need to make a lot of important decisions. Each of their decisions needs to be focused on making the profits of the company grow. Unfortunately, not all company leaders are created equal. Some of them make mistakes in making business decisions, some more than others. If the leadership of a company constantly makes mistakes, he could end up making the company lose money. The market also hates it when this happens.

When the leader of a listed company fails, the board of directors of that company may choose to change the leader. The market is generally interested with these types of events. When one of the companies that you are keeping track of is changing its CEO or president, you want to check the credentials of the person who will replace him or her. Usually, the board will assign a replacement who has experience in the industry. The type of replacement that a company hires in times like these says a lot about the plans that they have for the company in the future.

If the new CEO that a company hires for example, has a lot of experience in sales, then the company may be looking to increase its sales numbers. If the company hires a person who specializes in product development, then they may be planning to create new products to be added to their inventory.

Aside from the top dogs of the company, you also want to look into how well the company keeps its talents. When a company's employees, especially top level ones, stay in the company for a long time, this is a sign that the company is stable. The market likes it when there is stability in a company.

If the company has trouble keeping its top talents on the other hand, this may mean that there is something wrong with the company internally.

What is the company's market share?

The marker share is an important metric in the stock market. People generally want to invest in the companies that have the majority market share in the industries where they operate. It is a measure of the competitiveness of the business.

For companies that are already dominating their markets, they want to keep their market shares high. For a growing company on the other hand, they want to increase their previous market share.

Learning to Read Financial Reports

All the information we've discussed above are all discussed in the financial reports of the companies in the stock market. A company listed in the stock market is required to provide quarterly reports to their investors. These reports are submitted to the SEC. It is also posted in the company's corporate website. You want to access the financial reports of the companies that you are about to invest in. In particular, you want to look into the cash flow of the company.

The Cash Flow Statement

The cash flow is a document that shows how much money is coming into the company and how much of it is flowing out. A strong company has more money flowing in.

The Balance Sheet

Next, you want to look into the company's balance sheet. The balance sheet is the document that shows you a summary of the assets and liabilities of a company. When examining the balance sheet of the company, your primary focus is to find out the liquidity of the company. Liquidity refers to the amount of cash assets that a company owns. The liquidity can be measured by getting the current ratio. To compute for this ratio, let us first discuss the parts of a balance sheet.

Assets refer to the things or any type of resource that the company owns that gives it more value. There are three types of assets in a typical balance sheet, the current assets, the fixed assets and the financial assets.

Current assets are the type of assets that are likely to be converted to cash within the next business year. They include cash and cash equivalents, accounts receivable, inventory, and any prepaid expenses that the company may have. Fixed assets refer to permanent types of resources that are likely to be kept for a long period. This may include production plants, company machinery and equipment and real properties like buildings. Ideally, the fixed assets need to have a part in the business operations of a company. Financial assets are investments in the securities of other institutions. This type of assets is common among holding companies.

After checking out the assets of the company you are interested in, you may also want to check out their liabilities. Liabilities refer to the legal financial obligations of the company. In most cases, it refers to the debts that the company took on to fund their growth and business operations. There are also three common types of liabilities, the current, non-current, and contingent liabilities. Current Liabilities refer to debt that needs to be paid within one year. This type of liabilities needs to be given special consideration because they are more urgent than other types of liabilities.

Non-current liabilities are those that have a payment deadline of more than a year. These include long term debt and deferred tax liabilities, mortgage payments and leases. It's best that the company start paying off these types of liabilities even when they aren't as urgent as the current liabilities because they also carry an interest rate. If the interest rate of a non-current liability is too big, it will eat up much of the profits of the company.

Contingent liabilities are conditional types of liabilities. The company only needs to pay them if certain conditions are met. An example of this is when a company is facing a lawsuit. If they win the lawsuit, there is no need to face the liability. However, if they lose or if there is a settlement, the company may need to pay up. At this point, the contingent liability becomes either a current or non-current liability, depending on the outcome of the lawsuit.

Now that you know what the contents of the balance sheet are, you can now learn what the true value of the company is. The basic formula here is:

Assets = Liabilities + Shareholders' Equity

As you can see, there is a third part to this equation and that is the Shareholders' equity. This numbers refers to the equity held by all the shareholders of a company. In the beginning of a company, the shareholders' equity is made up of the money put up by the investors to help the founder of the company starts the business.

When a company earns money, it has a number of options. First off, it could pay off its debts. This will decrease the total liabilities of the company.

Next, it could use the earnings to pay off dividends. This is best done when there is no debt to be paid. Giving out dividends rewards the shareholders directly.

Lastly, the company can use their earnings by reinvesting it to the company. When this happens, the amount reinvested in the company is added to the shareholders' equity.

In theory, this money should help the company grow bigger. However, in reality, the money will only help the company if it is used in the right parts of the business. Aside from the capital and retained earnings, the shareholders' equity will also include the common stocks issued by the company.

When a company needs to liquidate its assets, the creditors are always paid first before the investors. The investors only get whatever is left after the assets has been liquidated and distributed to the creditors. For a balanced sheet to be truly balanced, the total assets should account for all the money borrowed (liabilities) and given by investors (shareholders' equity).

If the value of the assets is greater than the sum of the liabilities and the total equity of the company, this means that the company may have intangible assets that have not been added to the sheet.

On the other hand, if the liabilities and equities side is greater than the total value of the assets, then there is a problem with how that money has been used.

A company's statement of assets and liabilities changes often. A company acquires new assets all the time. As the company sells more of its products and services, it is expected to also gain more assets in cash and receivables. As the details in the balance sheet changes, so does the current ratio.

To get the current ratio, you will need to divide the current assets with the current liabilities. The current assets represent that amount of money that the company is guaranteed to receive in the next year. On the other hand, current liabilities refer to the debt that the company needs to pay in the next year. By dividing the current assets with the current liabilities, you can check if the liquid assets of the company are enough to pay off its financial obligations.

Financial author and investor Phil Town suggests that a strong company needs at least a current ratio 2:1 to be competitive. This ideal ratio is just a rule of thumb and it applies best towards small and medium corporations. Many blue chip companies survive with a lower liquidity ratio. You may choose not to use this standard in these companies.

On the other hand, if you are investing in small companies, you need them to have a good liquidity ratio. When doing fundamental analysis, the current or liquidity ratio tells you about the ability of the company to pay for its operations and debts. If the company has a ratio lower than 1:1 (the assets and liabilities being equal), this means that the company will deplete its liquid assets within the next year unless it acquires more cash. If the company has a 2:1 ratio on the other hand, it means that they may have at least another year to turn things around.

The Income Statement

The income statement provides information on the performance of a company in a given period. In a quarterly income statement for example, you can expect to see the amount that the company earned through its business operations for the entire quarter. A manufacturing company for instance may include the income that it got for selling its products.

Subtracted from the total sales number is the cost of goods sold. This is the amount used to produce the products that were sold. By subtracting the cost of goods from the sales numbers, you get the gross profit.

Next, the income statement may include the operating expense of a company. The operating expenses varies for each company. The bigger the company, the bigger its operating expenses will be. Some companies like holding companies can keep their expenses low because they do not need to spend more to earn a higher income.

By subtracting the operating expenses from the gross profit, you get the operating income. Some companies still need to deduct the interest expenses from this amount. The interest expenses refers to the payment that need to be made to pay off interests for any debt that the company may have. After this expense is deducted, you have the Income before Taxes. After finally deducting the taxes, you get the net income.

The income statement is a great tool for checking if the company is growing. When a company is listed in the stock market, it is expected to grow. The whole point of getting financing through a public listing is to make the company grow.

We can check if the company is growing by comparing the details of multiple income statements. In particular, you want to check three important metrics, the sales numbers, the operating expense and the net income. First, let's talk about the sales income. If the sales income is growing, this means that the company is doing the right things in marketing the product or service. It could also mean that the company has managed to infiltrate new markets. Regardless of the reasons why it happened, improved sales numbers is always good news for the company.

Next, you will need to compare past and present operating expenses. The changes in the operating expenses will depend on the changes applied by the company on its operations. For instance, hiring more people will lead to higher operating expenses. A higher operating expenses deducts from the total sales income but it is not always a bad thing. If the higher operating expense proportionately increased the income, then it may be justified.

Next, you want to check the net income. The net income is the most important number for most companies. Ideally, the sales income and the net income should grow together. If the sales income grows but the net income decreases, there is a good chance that either the operational expenses or the interest expenses increased.

Calculating the ROA

Now that you are familiar with the Income statement and the balance sheet, we will use one metric from each of these reports to get the Return on Assets or ROA. The ROA is a measure of efficiency. A company with a good ROA means that the company is using its assets efficiently to gain as much earnings as they can.

The ROA is calculated by dividing the net income by the total value of the company's assets. A strong company can get as much as an annual 30% ROA. This means that the company managed to increase its value by that rate in the given period.

You want to keep investing in companies that consistently get a high ROA. If the company keeps this metric up, this means that they will be profitable for a long time.

Examining the Cash Flow

The Cash Flow Statement is the third type of financial statement that companies usually released in their corporate websites. The cash flow statement is simply a declaration of how cash was used in a given period. In a cash flow statement, you will see a list of cash related activities including the operating activities, investing activities and the financing activities. To understand the cash flow, start by looking at the Beginning Cash Balance. This is a declaration of how much cash the company started with in the period. This amount is taken from the previous cash flow statement of the company.

Operating activities will show you all the cash gained and sold through business operations. If a company has some investment assets like selling of properties, it will gain some cash under its investment activities. This section however, will also reflect any investment assets bought by the company. If the company bought a truck for its operations for example, it will deducted in this section.

Lastly, the financing activity is the part of the cash flow statement that shows the cash gained or lost from other people and institutions. A company will have a positive value in this area if it got some cash through borrowing money or getting capital from investors. On the other hand, it will get a negative value in this section if it paid a part of its debt or if it gave out dividends.

Each of the activities may have a positive or negative net value. The total value that we get from the cash flow is then subtracted or added from the Beginning Cash Balance to get the Ending Cash Balance. A positive cash flow will increase the value of the cash balance. A negative cash flow on the other hand will lead to a decrease in the cash balance.

It is normal for a company to have a negative cash flow in the beginning of the business. However, for a company to survive, it needs to eventually have positive cash flow through its business activities.

Two things need to happen for a company to turn a negative cash flow into a positive one. First, it needs to start selling its products or services. The sales of the company will lead to more cash flowing in.

Second, the company needs to reduce its operating costs. This could be done through simple activities like conserving energy in the stored owned by the company or avoiding wastage of company resources. This could also be done through changes in the operations of the company. For instance, instead of creating their own products a company could have the products created in other countries with cheaper labor costs. The strategies used by the company depend of course on the goals and planning of the CEO and his or her team.

When looking at a company's cash flow statement for the first time, you need to compare their cash balance to the actual costs of maintaining their company. If the cost of maintaining the company every month is $1 million for example, and the company only has $20 million in cash, this means that they can only keep their business going for 20 months. This is a not a good sign for a company. In contrast, a company with a bigger cash balance and lower operational expenses will last much longer.

Using Ratios that Work for You

The details in the financial reports will already give you a lot of information about the company. If the company is doing well, you will easily see it in the financial reports. It's different when the company has something to hide. When a company is secretive, you will notice that they will only show details that they are required to show.

You will need to do your own analysis to check whether the company is good for investing or not. Financial analysts use ratios to find out more about a company. These ratios allow some people to find information that the company may include in their financial reports.

One of the most commonly used ratios is the P/E ratio (Price-earnings ratio or PER). This ratio is used to compare the Price of the stock to the company's earnings per share.

This is an example of a valuation ratio. Valuation ratios are used to get the true value of a stock. This kind of analysis assumes that the market is an inefficient one and that there are factors in the market that has yet to be reflected in a price. If we agree that the market is inefficient, we could assume that the market price does not always show the true value of the companies in the market and sometimes corrections happen. A valuation ratio like the PER allows investors to guess the true value of a company stock. They then compare this value to the stock price to guess whether the stock price is lower or greater than the true value.

Value investors use this information to know when to start buying stocks. Value investors try to look stocks whose price is below their true value. Each investor, however, has their own preferred ratio to use when doing investment valuations. If you want to use this strategy in picking stocks, it's best to research on the different ratios that other investors use.

Chapter 6 – Time Your Entry to the Market

"Spend each day trying to be a little wiser than you were when you woke up."

~Charlie Munger

After researching on the companies that you will invest in, it's time to pick a time to enter the market. Ideally, you want to enter when there is a dip in the price of the stocks you are buying. This will allow you to buy stocks at a discounted rate.

In this chapter, we will talk about the opportunities wherein you will be able to do this.

When should you start buying?

- Don't buy in a bull market

When the rest of the market is in the mood for buying shares, you will see the price of the most popular stocks rise. If the prices of the stocks you are going for has already risen a considerable amount, it's usually not a good idea to buy. A 5% to 10% rise in the price since the previous low price, for instance, usually means that short term traders have bought the particular stock.

- Using Technical Analysis to Time your Entry

Aside from fundamental analysis, you could also use technical analysis to pick a time to buy. While a fundamental analyst makes use of company information to make an investing decision, the technical analyst focuses solely on the price and its movements. In short, it is an analysis of the price of stocks and other securities. When using technical analysis, you are trying to make decisions based on the insights you get from these price movements.

To start your technical analysis in the market, you need to look at the overall price movement of the index or sector where your target stock is listed. If you are looking to buy Apple Inc. stocks for instance, you can go to the technology sector or even the computer manufacturing subsector to check the general movements of the stocks. This will give you an idea of the state of the general market. If Apple Inc.'s stock prices are going down together with the price of all the other computer manufacturing companies, you can assume there is an industry or sector wide problem that is preventing investors from buying. Ideally, you want to know what this issue is before making a purchase. If the issue can be remedied soon, the stock price movements and you may get a decent payday if you buy now. However, if the issue in the industry cannot be remedied, you are in danger of buying stocks in an industry with no chance of recovery.

Technical analysis is more of a trader's tool. It is usually used by short term traders. However, it can also be used by position investors who are in it for the long haul. If a company with great fundamentals is experiencing a blow in the market, you know that they will be able to recover. This is true for companies with great liquidity, a positive cash flow, a healthy growth rate and a great position in the market. If the stock prices of that company are going down, you may have a chance to enter a position for cheap.

While fundamental analysis will tell you if a company is good enough to invest in, technical analysis will tell you when the price is low enough for you to make a purchase. It allows you to spot trends, analyze these trends, and establish entry and exit points in your trades.

Reading Charts

Before you can do technical analysis, you first need to learn how to read a basic price chart. First, you will need to view the chart of your chosen company stock. Some brokers provide this feature in their trading platforms. The chart is basically a graph that shows you the movement of price over time. If you already have an account with a broker, you may look for the chart in the trading platform they provide.

If your broker does not provide this service, you can also look up a chart from the website of the stock exchange where your target company is listed. If you search your chosen company in the NYSE website for example, you will be led to a page that contains the price chart of the said company.

In a digital price chart like the ones you see in the NYSE website, you will be able to choose the type of chart plot to be displayed. Your options are the line plot, bar plot, area plot, dot plot, histogram plot, candlestick plot and the Heikin-Ashi plot. In this book, we encourage you to use both the candlestick plots and the Heikin-Ashi plots. Both plot types are useful for looking into trends. Let's start with a candlestick plot.

The Regular Candlestick Plot

The candlestick plot contains a body which is a rectangular shape. The body, when placed in a price chart represents the opening and the closing price for the period. In Western markets, the candlestick is green when the stock price closed at a higher price than its opening. In this case, the open price will be the bottom of the candlestick while the top will the close price.

A red candlestick indicates that the price of the stock is lower than its open price. This means that the stock value decreased over the period. In this case, the top part of the candlestick is the open price and the bottom is the close price.

You may also see lines extending above and below the body of the stick. These are called shadows and they indicate the extremes of the price fluctuations of the trading for the period.

If the candlestick is set to show daily prices, the shadow sticks will tell you of the highest and the lowest price of trading. The longer the shadows of the candle stick, the greater the price fluctuation is.

Candlestick plots are a great tool for spotting trends. When a particular stock is experiencing massive selling, you will see multiple successive red candlesticks. This is an example of a trend when the price is going down. When this happens, you want to know when the trend is going to hit the bottom and turn around. If the fundamentals of the company are great, the trend will eventually turn around.

When a particular stock is experiencing massive selloffs, you will see multiple successive red candlesticks. This is an example of a trend when the price is going down. When this happens, you want to know when the trend is going to hit the bottom and turn around. If the fundamentals of the company are great, the trend will eventually turn around. This is called the pivot point. You want to start buying when you start to see signs of this pivot points.

You will also see an upward trend using the candlestick plot. This looks like multiple green candlesticks with short upper shadows. Sometimes, there may not even be an upper shadow. When you see this kind of trend and you are not in a position, then buying may not be a good idea. You will make a lot of money as an investor when you enter a trade in the beginning of a trend or even before a trend begins. If you enter when the trend has already been going on, you run the risk of entering the trade too late. When this happens, you may just lose money when the trend turns around right after you took your position.

Heikin-Ashi Plot

The Heikin-Ashi plot is a variation of the candlestick. However, it uses a different set of formula for its open, close, high and low prices. Here are the formulas:

Close = (open + high + low + close) / 4

High = maximum of high, open, or close (whichever is highest)

Low = minimum of low, open, or close (whichever is lowest)

Open = (open of previous bar + close of previous bar) / 2

The high and low prices reflect the highest and lowest prices for the trading period. The close price represents an average between the open, high, low and close prices for the period. Lastly, the open price uses the average of the open and close prices of the previous period's bar.

What these changes do is that they make a smoother looking chart. While in a regular candlestick chart, you will often see alternating green and red in a single trend line, the Heikin-Ashi line will show you a consistently green or red line on a trend. For a Heikin-Ashi Candle stick to become red from being green, the average price of the open, close, high and low of the trading period must be lower than the average of the open and close of the previous bar. It will take a far greater dip for the Heikin-Ashi candlestick to reverse a trend.

For now though, focus on using a regular candlestick to get the hang of creating trend lines. The Heikin-Ashi plot will be useful when you have mastered the use of the regular candlestick.

Creating Trend Lines

A trend line is a line that shows a consistent direction of the price. It can be created by joining one price point to another in a price chart. A trend line is the prevailing direction of the price and every technical analyst wants to establish a valid trend line before making any trading decision.

To start creating a trend line, you will need to pick a company that you are interested in buying and pull up its price chart. Next, you will need to pick a period of time and a time frame. The period of time could be as long as five years or more or as short as a day.

Day traders use a shorter period when analyzing price. Long term investors on the other hand, views charts in terms of weeks, months or even years.

The timeframe on the other hand is the frequency on which the chart with break the bars. In a chart that shows the prices for the entire trading day for instance, you will see an hourly timeframe. It simply means that the bars in the chart represent the highs, lows, open and close for an hour of trading.

As a beginner, it is ideal to look into trades in a monthly period and a daily timeframe. You could even view them in periods longer than one month.

After selecting your settings for viewing the chart, your next step is to look at the current price movements. If there is a consistent successive green candlesticks before the current price, then you may be looking at an uptrend. If there is a collection of successive red candlesticks, you may be looking at a downtrend. In an uptrend or a downtrend, the body of the candlesticks is usually long, indicating that the company stock is traded in great volumes during the timeframe. If you see a red candlestick with a long body in a chart with an hourly timeframe, this means that in that time, there was a lot of volume sold at decreasing prices.

Picking a Starting Point

Each trend line has a starting point and a series of touches. The starting point is point in time in the chart where in the increasing or decreasing price patterns start. In our case, we want to use our analysis to know when to enter the market. Because of this, we are focused on knowing when a downward trend will end. In this case, you want to pick a starting point where in the price started going down.

It takes experience to accurately pick the correct starting point. Some analysts use a combination of fundamental analysis and technical analysis to identify these points. For instance, you may expect to see a dip in stock prices right after a company releases a disappointing financial report.

After picking a starting point, the next step is to draw a line from the starting point that touches the top of the body of another candlestick. If you are plotting a downward trend line, you are likely to draw a diagonal line that is going downward. Ideally, you want your trend line to touch the top of at least three candlesticks. There should be no other candlestick protruding over your downward trend line. This is called a breach in the trend line and when you have a breach on your downward trend line, this means that your line is invalid. For a downward trend line to be valid, it needs to have a start point, at least three touches from succeeding candlesticks and no candle stick is breaching the line.

You want to find a company with great fundamentals to have this kind of line. When you find this kind of company, you want to look into the news about it that will help explain the dip in the stock price. If the reason for the dip in the price can be reversed, it's just a matter of time before the stock prices start picking up again. You will know when this is about to happen when a long downward trend line is suddenly breached by a strong upward tick. Not all breaches will result to a reversal of trends. The breach needs to be strong and this will be represented by another candlestick with a long body. It could also be represented by simultaneously positive short candlesticks.

A consistent breach from an original trend line means that the bullish part of the market has emerged and started buying the stocks of the company. When the direction of the trend line was downwards, people were just waiting for it to breach to jump in and buy stocks. They were all waiting for the trend line to be breached just like you. If there are a lot of bullish people aiming to buy that company stock, you will see a massive reversal in the downward trend. People will start buying the stocks and hold their position until the peak of the upward trend is reached.

Support and Resistance Lines

There are two basic types of trend lines: the support and resistance lines. The support line is the trend line drawn below the candlestick. It acts as a line that tells the investors the bottom prices that most people are willing to pay for a stock. The resistance line on the other hand, is a trend line drawn above the candlestick. This shows the peak prices that people are willing to pay for the stock in the indicated periods.

An uptrend will show you a consistently increasing support and resistance line. The opposite is true in a downtrend.

Using Trend Lines to Time your Entry

In our goal to find the best time to buy in a down trend, we need to find when our valid resistance line is breached. You can start by drawing a line from the starting point or a high peak in the price chart. You could then draw a straight line between your starting point and the other price peaks in the down trend. When drawing these lines, make it touch the body and not the shadows of the candle. As we have discussed above, you want your trend line to be touched by the peaks of the downtrend at least three times.

These touches are signs of important market behavior. In a downtrend, a touch in the resistance line tells you that at a certain point, a group of investors bought a large enough volume of stocks to increase its price. However, some other group of investors used the opportunity to sell their own stocks to make profit. This tells you that there are people waiting for the price of the stocks to reach your resistance line before selling their positions.

If the fundamentals of a company are good, this will eventually turn around. This is called a pivot point. The pivot point is the point in time when a trend is likely to reverse. In this case, the expected reversal means that it is time to buy the stock. The price reversal indicates that the number of sellers for that particular stock has been exhausted. All the sellers have been satisfied and their presence will no longer stop the bulls in the market in driving the price up. You will know that it is about to turn around if there is a strong breach in your resistance line.

When it is breached by one long bodied candle or multiple short bodied candles, then you may assume that people are starting to buy at a higher price and a new trend is emerging because of the entry of the bullish buyers. This may be a start of a new uptrend trend line.

If you are using a long term investing strategy, you will often see trend lines change according to the news. If a breach is accompanied by a good news in the market, the upward movement will look stronger and it may actually last longer. This will translate to better profits if you chose to buy right after the breach.

Using Moving Averages as Buying Signals

The moving average is another price signal that is often used by technical analysts in making buying and selling decisions. It is calculated by taking the closing prices in the period specified in the calculation (50 days, 100 days, 200 days, etc.) and creating one average price. The average price is then plotted in the chart so that the moving averages create a line in the chart. This line is called the Simple Moving Average line

The simple moving average line is a great tool that will tell you if a particular stock price trend is about to turn around. One way to use it is by comparing the actual price movement to the moving average of a stock. If the price crosses the moving average, you can use that as a buy or sell signal. It's best to use a longer-term SMA when using this strategy (100-200 SMA).

However, using just one moving average may give you a weak signal and may not actually be indicative of what is actually happening in the market. For this reason, most investors most more than one moving averages. For example, you can use two moving averages and put them both on the same chart. One of the moving averages could be long term (example: 200-day SMA) and the other, short term (example: 50-day SMA).

The short term moving average line will be reactionary to the price changes. This means that you will see it go down as soon as the trend is going down. You will also see it go up as soon as the price creates a down trend.

The long term moving average on the other hand will look smoother, with fewer peaks and dips in price. It takes longer for this moving average to change its direction.

Technical analysts use at least two of these moving averages to create a stronger trend signal. If you are tracking a downtrend for example, you can use a moving average together with your other trend lines to help you decide when to buy. If the price patter crosses both these lines, that's a strong buying signal. It tells you that there are enough bulls in the market to change both the long term and the short term SMA lines. A trend shift like this has a lot of backing from the buyers in the market and it will last longer.

Other Advanced Buy Indicators

There are more hundreds of other buy and sell indicators used by the technical analysts in the market. If you find that technical analysis to be effective in your paper trades, you may choose to explore buy indicators like the different variations of the moving average and stochastics. These are some of the most popular types of buy indicators. Study them and apply them in your paper trades to check if they are reliable in the sectors and indices where you choose to operate.

Chapter 7 – Learning About Buy and Sell Orders

"Risk comes from not knowing what you are doing."

~Warren Buffett

Next to the process of picking stocks, beginners also often become intimidated with the actual buying and selling process. You will find few tutorials on how to actually buy and sell from you PC because of the lack of content in the subject. Those who are serious in investing don't really give a lot of their time on creating tutorials. The ones who do are usually unprofessional and don't give out enough details about the subject.

The actual buying and selling process will also depend on the order features of your broker's trading software. For security reasons, some of these brokers may choose to prohibit videos and images of actual buying and selling of stocks using their platform.

In this chapter, we will discuss the common features that are common in the online trading platforms. It's important to be familiar with these terms even before you start buying stocks. If you do forget about them, just return to this part of the book when you do start trading.

Basic Parts of a Buying Order

When buying stocks, the information you need includes the name of the stock, the amount of money that you want to invest and the lot size.

- The Name of the Stock

The name of the stock is represented by an abbreviation called a ticker symbol. When buying stocks, you will be able to search for the company stock you want from the broker's platform using this abbreviation.

Depending on the exchange, the symbol can be made up of two to six letters. It's best to look up the symbol of the company first from sources like NYSE.com, NASDAQ.com or the specific website of your chosen exchange.

Double check your ticker symbol before you make the purchase order to make sure that you don't order the stocks of the wrong company. Sometimes, the names of companies are very similar and it can be easy to make order mistakes.

- Purchase Amount

The amount of money that you are willing to use in a purchase order will depend on a number of factors. One of them will be your budget. Obviously, you will only be able to make a purchase order if you have the budget to meet the minimum purchase price.

The minimum purchase price will depend on two things, the board lot and the price of the company stock. The board lot is the minimum number of stocks that may be assigned to a particular stock by the broker. Not all brokers assign board lots however, the big ones do to prevent confusion. If your broker assigns board lots, this will make it easier for you to take note of your trades. The default lot size for most stocks is 100 units of stock. However, the brokerage firm changes the lot size based on the market price of the actual stock.

To check the minimum amount that you will need to buy stocks of a certain company, just multiply its minimum lot size to its market price. If the lot size is 100 shares for example and the price of a share is $1, then you will need a minimum of $100 to buy that company share.

When planning to buy the stocks of a certain company, you may want to look up this information as early as possible to help you create an informed purchasing decision.

- Stock Price (Bid)

Aside from your budget for the transaction, you also want to specify the stock price in which you will buy the stock. This will be your bid for the stock. This will specify the maximum buying price that you will accept for your stock. The price is one of the biggest determinants whether your order will be filled.

Let's say that a company stock that you want to buy is hovering at the $10 and $12 range. You decided that you will purchase that company stock if it goes below the $10 mark. In this case, you may be able to buy the stock at $9.90 or one tick below $10.

The moment your order is placed, it will be one of the orders in line for that particular bid price. Other orders that specified a higher bit will be executed first even if they were placed later than your order. Your bid price will only be reached if there are no other orders that can be filled at a higher bid price.

If the price does reach $9.90, all the orders in line in that price will be executed according to the number of stocks available in the market. The orders that were placed first will be executed first among orders that have the same bid.

If it is your order's turn to be executed, your bid price will be matched to the asking price of the sell orders in the market. If there is someone selling their stocks at $9.90 or below that fits your other order specifications, your order will be filled.

If your bid is too low, it is possible that your order will not be executed because there are not sellers with an asking price as low as your bid price.

- The Lot Size

Lastly, you will need to specify the number of shares that you will actually buy. When you are starting out, it's best to stick to the minimum amount in your first few purchases. If you do decide to go over the minimum lot size, you will need to make sure that you have allocated enough for the amount of stocks that you are going to buy.

Buy Limit Orders

Most broker trading software programs nowadays also come with additional order command features. These features are not present with all broker software however, so it would be advantageous if you choose a broker that does provide them. These additional purchase order features help specify to the brokerage firm how you want your order to be executed.

Here are some of the commonly used buy limit orders:

- Day

One of the order commands that you can add to your order is the Day option. When you create a Day order, it tells the broker to fill the entire order before the end of the trading day. If the day order is not filled when the day ends, the unfilled portion of the order will be automatically cancelled.

This is the default command in most trading platforms. A variation of this order is the Day + order wherein the order remains active if there is an extension in the trading period for the trading day. The Day order is one of the duration type orders.

- Fill-or-Kill (FOK)

When you execute this order, the brokerage will immediately send out your order. If there are sellers willing to fill your purchase order entirely, it will be filled. However, if there aren't any, your order will be automatically cancelled.

With this type of order, your broker will not attempt to partially fill your order. If there is no immediate seller who can fulfill it entirely, your order will be "killed". This is done immediately after the order is placed.

- All or None (AON)

Just like the FOK order, the AON limit requires the broker to attempt fill the entire order or cancel the entire transaction altogether. However, this type of order can be assigned with other duration limits to extend its lifespan. For example, you could assign an AON order together with a DAY order to tell the broker to execute an AON order that will last for the entire day. By the end of the trading day, your order will either be completely filled or cancelled.

Some traders to not want to buy certain stocks unless they can get a minimum amount. This is especially useful when you are working with the last portions of your budget. Either you will get the entire amount of stocks that you specified in the purchase order or you will get nothing at all.

- Immediate or Cancelled (IOC)

If you want to make an order in real time, you can use the IOC limit. This type of order indicates to the broker to fill the order or cancel the unfulfilled portion immediately.

The IOC order allows for only a part of your order to be filled unlike the FOK order that requires the broker to fill the entire order amount. If your order is filled halfway in the first attempt to execute it, you will only get that much of a particular stock. The other half of the order will be cancelled or "killed".

- Good 'til Cancelled (GTC)

The GTC order is another duration order where in the broker will continue to try to execute the order until it is cancelled in your account. With this type of limit, your order will continue indefinitely until you cancel it.

This can be useful if you are trying to get a certain stock for a bargain price. You can just keep your order going until the stock price dips to the level that you like.

- Good 'til Day (GTD)

The GTD limit is used when you want your order to last multiple trading days. It is followed by a specific date when you want the order to be cancelled if it is not filled. In contrast, the day order always ends at the end of the trading day when it is created.

- At the Opening (OPG)

OPG limit specifies to your broker to execute the order at the start of a trading session. If it is not filled immediately at the first attempt, it will be killed.

- At the Closing (CLO)

The CLO limit is just like the OPG but it is executed at the end of the trading sessions instead.

Creating a Sell Order

If you are already holding a number of company stocks, your next step is to decide when you will sell them. In our example above, you bought stocks at a price of $9.90. You want to sell it for a profit so you need to decide on the price.

Just like when buying stocks, you also need to specify the number of stocks that you will sell and the price that you will sell it in. The amount of stocks that you will sell is also limited by the minimum lot size indicated by your broker.

Just like when buying, the execution of your sell order will also be limited by your selling price, called the "Ask", and the available bids in the market. Most beginners make the mistake of creating orders with an extremely high asking price. It takes a bit of technical analysis and experience to know the best asking price for a particular stock.

If your asking price is too high, it may take too long for your sell order to be executed. If you placed a duration limit on your sell order, your order may expire before it is filled.

It is also important to note though that any gains or losses you get in the market will not be finalized until you actually sell your position. For this reason, it helps not to be overly reactive to the events in the market. If the stock prices of the shares you bought dipped, do not panic and sell immediately. As mentioned this will transform your losses from being "paper" losses to reality.

At the same time, you also want to avoid holding on too long on your positions. If you have reached your financial goals, immediately sell your stocks while people are still buying at a high bid. You also need to anticipate any discrepancy in the price of the stocks and its actual value. This is common when there is a lot of hype surrounding a particular stock. Most stocks begin at a low price or an undervalued rate. This is when you want to buy. As the stock price grows, the stock begins to become overvalued. This happens when there are a lot of people who wants to buy the stock of a company.

Strategies for Placing Orders

The worst possible scenario when placing an order is for your order not to be executed by the system because your price may be too low when buying or too high when selling. It's alright for this to happen if you don't feel a sense of urgency to complete the transaction. In this case, you can set your price any way you want. However, if you feel strongly that there is a need to complete a buy or sell order, you need to have a strategy in setting your ask or your bid.

Common Bidding Mistake

It's common sense for a beginner trader to make the mistake of bidding too low. Even a beginner technical analyst can make this mistake. In a beginner's first few trades, he or she may experience not filling orders because of this mistake. This happens when people become too cautious in the market. They take the adage "buy low and sell high" too seriously.

The danger with trading too low is that you may miss out on some of the best deals in the market because the price would not go as low as you would hope. In the previous chapter, we talked about using technical analysis to find an entry price to a trade. We talked about using a resistance and support trade lines to learn about the behavior of the traders in the market.In bidding, we usually use the resistance line as a way to tell whether the downtrend is about to break. A common mistake is to bid at a time right before the breach. This is as mistake because no one can accurately tell with one hundred percent certainty that a breach is about to happen before it actually happens. Beginner traders and some hyper aggressive traders may take the risk of calling when the breach will happen and make their trading decisions on that guess.

The mistake here is to decide on a bidding price before the breach in the resistance line happens. As a beginner trader, you should only make an order above the breach point, especially on highly profitable trades. While you will lose some profit in some deals, this strategy ensures that you will not miss out on buying a high-value company for a low price.

Common Selling Mistake

When selling, it is also common for inexperienced traders to set their price to high, in the hopes of maximizing their profits. Just like when buying, this mistake can cost a person to miss out on all the profits when the price peaks. The trader or investor may need to wait longer for another opportunity to sell. The time lost in a lost selling opportunity can also lead to opportunity lost. By missing to liquidate a set of assets ripe for selling, a trader may lose the opportunity to bid on other high value stocks in the market.

Asking a price that is too high can also happen because of speculation. When we speculate, we make high risk guesses without strong evidence when making our trading decision. These high risk decisions have a lower chance of being right when compared with tested and proven trading techniques.

You can lessen the chance of making a wrong decision by waiting for the price to breach the support line before selling your stocks. Another option is to sell your stocks when you have reached your financial goal. If you miss a selling opportunity though, your only two options are either to give up your position at a lower price and take a lower amount of profit or to wait until the price goes back up.

Deciding between the two can also be difficult. The general rule is to sell your position if you have other prospect company stock to buy. You will need to do this especially if the company stocks you are trying to sell are projected to be in a downtrend in a while. It could also be a good idea if the price of stocks is projected to go sideways.

Holding on the other hand, is better when there is still a lot of buzz in the company you are holding. You may profit some more by holding if you are anticipating positive news about the company's fundamentals.

Holding, however, further exposes you to more risks. Make sure that you know everything there is to know about the company before deciding to hold. Also make sure that you are aware of the possible consequences of holding.

Chapter 8 – Diversifying your Asset Distribution

"Searching for companies is like looking for grubs under rocks: if you turn over 10 rocks you'll likely find one grub; if you turn over 20 rocks you'll find two."

~Peter Lynch

Diversification is the process of spreading your capital to different types of assets to minimize the risk of losing money. Investing solely in the stock market exposes your capital to the specific risks associated in the stock market. If your investment activity for example, is focused on the automobile industry in the stock market, you run the risk of losing a big chunk of your capital if that industry tanks.

By spreading your wealth into different types of investment vehicles, you prevent one types of risk from wiping out your entire value of your portfolio. Here are some strategies that you can use to diversify your asset distribution:

- Investing in Other Sectors

If your portfolio value is still small, you may consider diversifying by investing in the other sectors. When selecting a new sector to invest in, you may use the method we discussed in previous chapters. Make sure that you learn about the new sector first and the companies in it before you actually pull the trigger.

Investing in a second sector widens your circle of competence. It increases the amount of companies that you can invest in safely. It also allows you to spread your funds to another industry so that you will be able to avoid exposing your money to one type of sector related risk.

One way to do this is by dividing your portfolio fund into two. You could leave one of the funds in the sector you first invested in. You could then distribute the other half in the new sector you've selected.

You could also go about it by leaving your old positions alone and investing only new funds into the new sector. This strategy is better if you are in no position of selling your older positions. With this strategy, you will be building up your fund in the new sector from scratch.

- Index Investing

Index investing is another strategy that you can use to diversify your fund's distribution. With this method of investing, you no longer need to spend too much time doing fundamental analysis. Instead, you only spread your wealth among the companies in the index you have chosen. For example, you could choose to use your funds to invest on the top companies in the S&P 500. You have a number of ways on how you can do this.

This method of investing is used by people who believe that it is impossible to constantly beat the market. This belief has some statistical backing. In the year 2010, more than 90% of fund managers failed to beat the performance of the S&P 500. The majority of the managers who did beat the market were in big hedge funds, mutual funds and banks that were only accessible to the rich. Because you are a beginner, we could assume that you will not be able to beat the performance of the market in your first year of trading. If you believe this too, you may be better of using the index investing method.

The first one requires a huge sum of money to get started. This strategy requires you to invest on the individual companies in your chosen index yourself. Pulling this off though can be difficult. You will need to invest a percentage of your fund on a company in your chosen index according to its weight in that index. Because the companies in an index are usually blue chip companies, you can expect some of them to have a high price. The board lot requirement for some of these expensive company stocks will prevent you from buying just the right amount to hit the sweet percentage of investment that corresponds to its weight in the index.

It will also be difficult for you to keep track of the changes in the index. The weight of each company in an index changes every time the prices of the companies change. This happens every trading day. You will also need to redistribute your own funds in these stocks every week or month so that your investment follows the weight distribution in the index.

If you do not want to keep track of an index and you don't want to go through the hassle of constantly adjusting the distribution of your investments, you could also opt to buy index funds. Index funds are a type of mutual funds that are specialized to mimic the distribution of an index in the market. Index funds are expected to have some fees though because they are run by an investing company.

To invest in an index fund, you will need to pick a company to invest in. You could then ask them if they are offering index funds. The best time to start investing in an index fund is when the market is doing well. Index funds tend to be of higher risk compared to other types of mutual funds. They are riskier than other types of managed funds like balanced funds and equity funds because of the tendency of its price to fluctuate. However, this higher risk is directly proportional to the potential rewards that you may get.

- Investing in other types of securities

If your goal is to maximize your diversification, you could also consider investing outside of the stock market. If your funds are totally invested in the stock market, you are exposing 100% of it to stock market related risks. As your funds grow bigger, you may want to put some of it in other types of securities. One option that you may consider is bonds. While company stocks are considered as equity investments, bonds are considered debt investments. The companies and government agencies who issue these bonds are basically borrowing money from you. The bond is the proof of the transaction and it states the amount of money borrowed, the schedule of repayment and the interest rate of the loan.

Aside from bonds, you may also choose to invest in commodities. Commodities trading applies a similar trading strategy as stocks, in that it requires you to buy low and sell high. However, instead of buying company stocks, you are buying and selling rights to certain amounts of a type of commodity (like gold, coffee, tobacco, etc.). These commodities usually come from other parts of the world and are sold in the US.

While the principle of investing is virtually the same, the style of trading is different.

- Investing in Real Properties

If your fund grows in value, you may also have the opportunity to invest in properties. Investing in another type of asset, one that is tangible, can increase the diversity of your asset distribution.

Investing in real estate though, just like any type of investment, requires you to study what you are buying. You also need to time your entry into the market.

If the price of real estate in your area is low compared to its potential value, you may choose to use it as your method of diversifying your income. There are multiple ways that you can earn through real estate investing. Just like with securities, you can also buy and sell properties. You also have the option of renting your properties out.

Chapter 9 – Planning an Exit Strategy

"It's not whether you're right or wrong that's important, but how much money you make when you're right and how much you lose when you're wrong."

~George Soros

Each transaction you have in the stock market and in your other types of investments need to have an exit strategy. This is a set of conditions that will help guide you on when to exit a trade.

Basing Your Exit Strategy On The Price

The price of the securities is one of the most important parts of investing. Just like when you buy your stocks, you can also use the price as your basis for selling your shares. If you bought your stocks for $10 per share for instance and your technical analysis tells you that there will likely be a resistance at $15, you can choose to have a sell order ready when the price reaches $14.50 or whatever the tick size is for that particular stock. In this case, you will have a maximum $4.50 profit before fees.

The price is also an important basis that you can use or setting the stop loss. The stop loss is a trading feature that allows you to sell your positions automatically if the price goes down a certain amount. One way to set a price for the stop loss is by setting a support line. You can set the stop loss order a few ticks just below the support line so that your position will be automatically sold when the support line is completely breached.

These simple price criteria will increase the likelihood that you will make money. It will also prevent you from losing more money than necessary.

Using Fundamentals to Guide Your Exit

Aside from the support line and the resistance line, you can also choose to let go of your trading positions after certain news and financial documents are released. If your information about the company tells you that their business has done well in the last quarter, you can expect the news to have favorable results. This is a good time to exit your trade with a profit.

This strategy however, may hurt you if the news and financial reports have a negative effect on the price of the company. It's best to use this strategy together with the price strategy to increase its chances of success.

Basing Your Decision On Your Financial Goals

Another basis that you can use in selling your positions is your financial goals. Always be aware of your financial goal. Each trade you make should help you inch closer towards that goal.

Let's say that you currently have $10,000 in your portfolio and your goal is to make it grow to $20,000 in the next five years. Since your goal is a 100% growth and you still have five years to work with, you can aim for high risk and high reward companies. This term is usually used for smaller companies that have a potential for growth. You could then exit each trade in these types of companies after making 8-10% gains. You will be able to reach your target amount if you enter the market at the right time and if you have the discipline to pull your money out when you get your gains.

Remember that as long as you keep your money in the market, you are also keeping it exposed to risks. You want to avoid unnecessary risks by exiting your trades when you have reached your goals.

Using Technical Analysis To Signal Your Exit

In the previous chapters, we used tools like the resistance, support and the SMA lines to signal the point on when we will buy our stocks. We could also do the same to signal our exit from the market.

The other exit signals that we've discussed in this chapter only work if your positions reach their target prices. However, in reality, you will often see the stock prices fluctuate before actually reaching your target price.

Sometimes, the trend will completely reverse before this point. If this happens to you, you may not be able to sell your positions if you only base your decision in the above criteria.

Some of the technical analysis terms that we've already discussed in previous chapters can help you in making you more decisive in the market. Let's start with the support lines.

Support line

The support line is a great tool to use for your exit strategy in a fluctuating market. The support is the price trend line that we draw below the candlestick. In an uptrend, the support line is an indication when the trend will stop. The price trend will continue to go up until the number of buyers for a certain stock is depleted and is overran by the sellers. The breach in the support line can signal that an uptrend is about to end.

In most cases, you will see touches on the support line, especially in whole-dollar prices. However, if the trend is strong, these touches will be accompanied by quick reversal. This is an indication that there are still buyers of the stock in the market that is preventing your stock from dipping too low. Every time it reaches a low point, people start buying into the stock.

The number of people who keep buying the stocks however, will eventually start to dwindle. At this point, you will see a price fluctuation and a breach in the support line.

This signal is particularly useful when you are thinking of when to sell your stocks before your goal or target price is reached. If there is a strong breach in the support line, you may consider selling even if the stock price is not near your target price.

Using the SMA as a Selling Signal

You can do the same strategy using the Simple Moving Average. When we were looking for buying signals, we used two moving averages in different duration criterial to determine when to buy. You can use the same method when determining your selling price.

In our example in previous chapters, we suggested a combination of the 50-day and the 200-day moving average. A more reactionary SMA combination may be needed when you are looking to sell. You could choose to use a 100-day SMA together with your 50-day SMA.

The strategy of using it to sell is pretty much the same with the support line. The SMA line will follow just below the price in an uptrend. When looking for a selling signal, you are waiting for the price to dip below both of your SMA lines.

Chapter 10 – Be Aware of the Cycles in the Market

"The four most dangerous words in investing are: 'this time it's different.'"

~Sir John Templeton

The stock market is a legal way of gaining money without working for it. Because of the opportunities it presents, it attracts investors from all walks of life – from those who are investing for their retirement to those who are in it for the short term gains.

With the massive amounts of people investing in the stock market, the events in the market is heavily affected by the nature of the masses. Many of the people buying and selling in the market do not really study the assets they are buying. Many beginner investors, in an effort to make many deals in a short time, only rely on technical analysis and fail to do any fundamental analysis in the trades they are making.

Because of the massive numbers and the diversity of people participating in the market, it is common to see pattern of trading behavior. These patterns happen because when a considerable amount of people in the market have the same ideas and these similar ideas lead to similar trading strategies and decisions.

One example of the use of patterns in the stock market is stated in the saying "Sell in May and Go Away". The saying indicates that growth in the market starts to happen around Halloween and ends in May. It indicates that after selling in May, holding of stocks from June to September is futile because of the lack of market growth at this time. While no study proves this theory, it is a common perception that cycles in the market exist and it's best to be aware of them when investing.

In this chapter, we will discuss some of the stock market patterns that do have statistical backing.

The January Effect

In the past, there was a theory that the price of stocks always rise on January of every year. There was a time when this was true. The increased rate of spending during the holidays increased the investing capital of both people and businesses. It was also a time when people put their earnings of the previous year towards their retirement funds and other institutional investing firms.

However, when this pattern was introduced, many traders started anticipating the January effect. As a result, more people started buying during December, before the January effect happens. They then try to sell during January when the anticipated January effect is in full swing.

The reaction of the market to the January effect however, changed the pattern. Instead of rising on January, the prices of popular stocks dropped during this time dropped because of the massive selloff. On the other hand, a new pattern of the price increasing during December started.

The January effect tells us that short term patterns are only reliable if the general investing public is not aware of it. Once the public gets a whiff of the pattern, they try to use it to their advantage to make short term profits. This messes up the pattern, making it less reliable.

United States Presidential Election Cycle

The United States presidential election cycle is a theory that states that the stock market is weakest during a president's first year in office. Yale Hirsch, the proponent of this theory suggests that in a president's first year, the work of the president is not usually focused towards the strengthening of the economy. He said that it is common for a president to focus on social welfare improvements and amending the tax laws at this time because these were the types of bills that take a long time to pass through congress.

The theory further states that the second year of the president's term may not be better than the first. Hirsch states that the recovery starts in the third year of the president's term and continues until the last year. Hirsch explains that this happens when the president tries to work to gain favors in the midterm election and the election for his second term in office.

The theory has been reliable for the early part of the century. However, it wasn't entirely reliable among many presidents from 1970s to the 2000s. Among the presidents whose first year marked a strong stock market performance are Franklin D. Roosevelt, George H.W. Bush, Bill Clinton, Barrack Obama and Donald Trump.

The Ray Dalio Model of Debt Cycles

Ray Dalio is one investor who expressed strong belief on the existence of market cycles. In a 31-minute YouTube video he used to market his book back in 2003, Dalio tried to explain in simple terms how the economic machine works and how he used this knowledge to avoid the 2008 stock market meltdown.

In this video, Dalio states that there are two important economic cycles happening in the stock market. He explains that there is a short term debt cycle and a long term debt cycle and both are driven by human nature at work in the financial markets.

Dalio states that a strong economy the one in the US, leads to constant productivity growth. This happens when companies gain capital to innovate and improve their productivity and therefore their profitability.

Unfortunately, the market likes to push the limits of productivity by using leverage or loans. Dalio states that when the economy is doing extremely well, a large part of the economic performance is driven by debt.

In the beginning, the debt in the economy starts small. Most of the businesses are not operating based on debt. Instead, they are operating based on equity. Certain economic conditions however, encourage people and businesses to take on debt. One condition is a low interest rate. The central bank of a country generally has complete control over the interest rate. In the US, it is called the Federal interest rate and it is controlled by the Federal Reserves.

The Short Term Debt Cycle

When the economy seems to be growing too slowly, the Federal Reserves may choose to decrease interest rates. This in turn, decreases the interest rates in banks and other lending institutions. You can think of interest rates as the cost of borrowing money. Some types of debt can have interest rates as low as 1%. Others can be as high as 10%. The low interest rate climate will encourage business owners to use debt to fund their business.

Over time, interest rates are left unchanged, and the overall debt in the economy grows. However, because of there is more cash in the economy created by all the debt, it looks like the market is booming. Debt increases spending and spending allows the money created by debt to spread to other industries. The extra money in the economy drives the economic growth.

The increase in the debt levels in one major industry can trickle down to other parts of the economy. When a large amount of debt money goes into the stock market, it is distributed to other participants of the stock market.

In the 2008, stock market crash a huge amount of the money injected into the stock market came from the mortgage and housing market. There was a massive debt bubble in the housing market because people were borrowing money to buy homes that they cannot afford or refinancing their mortgages to get cash for their lifestyle expenses.

In a debt driven economy like this, the boom always has an end. The end comes when the debt bubble is discovered.

In contrast, growth without debt is mostly driven by productivity. Productivity is a general term used to describe work and innovation. When a person or a business works and is innovative, they are rewarded with income or revenue. Productivity determines the growth of income or revenue over time.

Debt fast tracks productivity by providing the person or the business with the cash they need to get what they want. In a business setting, the borrowed money is used to grow the assets of the business. It is used to obtain production and fixed assets that improve the productivity of a company. The increased productivity, will lead to higher income this will lead to better wages, better stock prices and an image of a strong company.

When most companies appear strong because of the high amount of debt in the economy, this creates the rise in the debt cycle. In Dalio's model, he compares the productivity line to the short term and the long term debt cycles. When the debt grows, it artificially increases productivity. However, this is balanced out by the liability that the debtor needs to repay.

All types of debt need to be repaid sooner or later. It is during the payment time when the debt cycle tends to dip. When a person or a business borrows money, they are not just borrowing from the lender but also from their future selves. The business that borrows money from the bank will need to repay that liability with its future revenue. When it is paying off this debt and it can no longer borrow money, its productivity becomes stagnant and this marks the slowing down of the growth of a business.

Multiple businesses go through this type of cycle. They borrow money to increase productivity. When the borrowing stops and the payment phase starts, the productivity of the company no longer grows and the company goes through a period of tightening its belt to pay off its debts. Now, imagine if the thousands of companies that make up the economy go through the same cycle. The time when all the companies are trying to pay off debt becomes the slow growth phase in the debt cycle called the recession. On the other hand, the time when all the companies are borrowing money and aggressively growing marks the growth phase of the debt cycle called the expansion.

Expansions and recessions make up the two phases of the short term debt cycle and the process can happen in a span of 8-10 years. Every 8 years or so, we experience periods of great growth and a periods of paying off debt. During the expansion stage, the interest rates decrease, encouraging people and businesses to borrow money. The increased rate of spending brought about by this policy leads to inflation or the general increase in the price of goods in the market. When the inflation goes up too high, the Feds try to slow the economy down by increasing interest rates. The increased interest rate leads to the recession phase of the short term debt cycle.

The increased interest rates often fix the problem of inflation. When the inflation problem is fixed, the Feds lower the interest rates again to speed up the rate of growth of the economy. The lowered rates encourages borrowing again. The short term debt cycle starts all over again with the expansion stage.

The Long Term Debt Cycle

The short term debt cycle may fix the problem with inflation but it doesn't necessarily get rid of all the debt in the system. The recessionary phase of the short term debt cycle only slows down the debt growth. However, by the time a short term debt cycle is over, there is still debt left in the economy.

Because of this, the amount of debt in the economy continues to grow even with the Feds' interference. Over time, debt grows with the growth of the economy. Unfortunately, most people do not see the debt. They only see the growth in the economy. They are more focused on the great things happening around them like the growth of their business, the increase in their income or the rise in the values of their assets. This growth can be seen directly in the rise of the values of the different indices in the stock market. People are only looking at the economic boom. Most of them are not aware that most of this growth comes from the extreme amount of debt in the economy.

Over the decades, the rate of growth of debt in the economy increases. This can be offset by the increase in productivity and income in the private sector. However, the amount of unpaid debt accumulates over the decades that the economy is booming. When the growth of debt in the economy grows faster than productivity and income, the debt burden begins to take its toll on the economy.

The boom usually continues to happen until the whistle is blown on bubbles in the economy. The growth that debt created in the economy stimulated income and productivity also encouraged overspending. When people start to feel rich, they also increase their lifestyle spending. This allows the luxury industries to grow as well. The increased spending rate creates a bubble in the economy.

When the amount of debt in one part of economy becomes too big, some people begin to take notice. In the case of the 2008 housing market crash, there were already telltale signs of a bubble. Companies related to the mortgage industry kept growing. However, their growth was based on the sales of houses which are mostly facilitated through debt. The lack of regulation in the market also allowed people with bad credit to buy houses. These include people who have no means of paying off their mortgage.

The problem arose when people who bought houses failed to cover their monthly payments. Mortgage defaults started to increase. This means that the people who bought these houses declared that they could no longer pay for the house. Their homes were taken away and the credit created, which the lending companies considered as assets, vanish. Just like that the growth created by the debt-facilitated home sales also vanished. The bubble popped in the later part of 2007 and it continued to affect the economy for more than five years.

To Dalio, this is an example of the two parts of the long term debt cycle. In a long term debt cycle, the expansion leads to the creation and the accumulation of debt. When the debt burden grows too big, the economy correct itself in many different ways. The popping of an economic bubble is just one of them. It could happen through regulations like deleveraging. In a deleveraging, the government try to squeeze policies to slow down the economic machine. The debt burden also has an effect on the people. They lessen their spending to be able to pay off most of their debts. This creates a domino effect of incomes falling, disappearance of credit assets, decreased rate of borrowing, decreased asset prices and an eventual crash of the stock market and other high risk investment platforms.

In a deleveraging, people want to sell their assets to try to preserve the profits it gained over the years. However, the rush of people to sell their assets increases the supply of assets in the market and this drives the price down. This is the reason why many types of stocks, even those of fundamentally sound companies, take a beating in the stock market.

When this happens, lowering of the interest rate no longer has an effect on the economy. It is during these times that the interest rates reach the bottom at 0%. This kind of event happens rarely. Most people are lucky to see two deleveraging events in their lifetimes. However, it is an inevitable event for debt driven markets of most countries that practice the free market system.

A deleveraging is followed by measures to try to rehabilitate the economy. Businesses and individuals act independently to try to reduce their own debts and to preserve the value of their own assets. Some try to cut spending, pay off debt, or improve productivity. The government also plays a big part in the rehabilitation of the economy through redistribution of wealth and printing of money. These measures need to be balanced. With proper policies, the economy improves. It does take time but things do get better. Ray Dalio approximates the entire long term debt cycle to span 50 to 70 years. When the economic issues are fixed however, the cycle starts all over again. This time, a new generation of consumers, businesses, and investors take part in the start of the new cycle.

Investing Implications of the Debt Cycles

Knowing where we are in the debt cycle can help us in our decision making process when investing. The debt cycle teaches us to wary when there is too much buzz in the market. It tells us that high rate of growth is not always a good thing. Sometimes, it can even be interpreted as a symptom of a system issue in the economy.

More importantly, it tells us that it is normal to see ups and downs in the market. The sheer number of people in the market makes it an unpredictable system. However, by exploring the behavior of the participants of the market in the past, we may be able to make sense of the things happening now and the anticipate some of the events that may happen in the future.

One example of this is the anticipation that many people have today of the next stock market crash. People are expecting any type of boom in the market to be the beginning of another cycle. Many of them are looking into debt bubbles in the economy that may pop. Because of this, we may see these types of bubbles to be identified earlier. There will be some types of bubbles that are harder to find and human nature will continue to keep increasing the debt burden in the economy. Because we, as individuals cannot do anything about it, the best thing we could do is to protect our own assets when we see these bubbles arise. Make sure that you are no longer in the market when the bubble pops.

Chapter 11 – Common Investing Mistakes by Beginners

"The investor's chief problem -- even his worst enemy -- is likely to be himself."

~Benjamin Graham

You are most prone to make mistakes and take losses in the first year of your investing venture. This is when you are just trying things out. Beginners are more likely to be indecisive and fail to practice the best practices.

In this chapter, we will talk about some of the common types of mistakes that other beginners make. The goal is to learn about them and to avoid them.

- Not considering the amount of risk that they are taking

It is common for beginners to focus on the possible positive outcomes when thinking about their investments. They usually do not think about the possibility that they will lose money.

With this kind of mindset, people end up not thinking about the risk that they are exposing their money to. This is the reason why people still keep their positions even when there are signs that they should pull their money out. The euphoria that comes with the boom in the market affects their decision making process.

There are many types of risks that come with investing. There is always the possibility for example, that you are putting your money on the wrong company. There are also some types of risks that are associated with the entire market itself.

You need to assess these risks every day that you are invested in companies in the stock market. Make sure to only take on an amount of risk that you are comfortable with. You could base this on your personal risk tolerance that we talked about in previous chapters. You are the best judge of your personal risk tolerance. If investing heavily in the stock market makes you uncomfortable, you need to adjust your fund allocation to make sure to bring your investing amounts into comfortable levels.

- Investing too much of their money

One of the biggest mistakes that people do when investing is when they put too much of their money at risk in the market. It is common for regular investors to take a high risk approach when investing. If you invest all the money you have, you are putting pretty much your entire life on the line. It is not sustainable to do this because there will be a time when you will make the wrong trading decision.

To make sure that the rest of your life continues even though you are wrong in your investing decisions, you need to avoid betting your entire life savings on the stock market. Ideally, you want to keep only 50% to 80% of your savings on the stock market. You can choose to put the rest in a less risky type of investment like bonds of money market funds.

You need to reallocate a bigger amount outside of the stock market especially when you suspect that there is a bubble in the market. You can anticipate these bubbles by studying the different sectors that are taking in the most growth. If you suspect that the growth in a certain sector or even the entire economy is not sustainable, sell some of your positions in the stock market and transfer it to a safe haven like money market funds or precious metals.

- Not Diversifying

It's alright not to diversify when your funds are still small. Most people who are starting out, cannot even make the minimum purchase of some of the biggest companies because they cannot make the board lot.

However, as your fund grows in value, you will need to ensure that you protect it from all types of risks. You can do this through diversification.

It may be tempting not to diversify when your concentration in one company or one sector has proven to be effective in the past. This strategy however, is unnecessarily riskier than diversification.

One of the biggest reasons why people with large sums to invest do not diversify is because they do not have the time to do fundamental analysis on stocks of other sectors. Some also say that they do not diversify because they don't think doing will result to better gains.

Diversifying your asset distribution is not only a defensive strategy but also an expansionary one. It allows you to explore other opportunities in the market and in other securities and other investment opportunities. You might just find your investment gold nugget by doing it.

- Investing in companies they know nothing about

Each company in the stock market has a business behind it. The best determinants whether a company stocks will continue boils down to two basic business questions:

Does the business make money?

How much of the money it is making is it able to keep?

Companies that are listed in the stock exchange are held at a higher standard compared to private companies. They are also put under a higher level of scrutiny. Each company needs to do a balancing act between being aggressive in making the company grow and in avoiding risky moves that would make the company less profitable.

It is guaranteed that companies that submit awful financial reports end up losing value in the stock market. You need to see the signs of the business management ability of a company before you actually spend money on them.

- Extremely short-term Trading

Investing is meant to be a long term activity. The people who created and traded the first stocks probably did not think that the ownership of equities of a company will be bought and sold within a day.

The people who buy and sell stocks within a day are not investors; they are speculators. Strategies like these never actually outdo the performance of the market or any of the trade indices.

Short term traders do not do well because it is impossible to be always correct in an unpredictably volatile market. It's better to stick to medium term and long term investment strategies. With these strategies, you are not just reacting to the market.

Instead, all your actions and decisions are based on actionable information derived from the market. Long term trading strategies also give you more time to adjust your strategies. It takes away the extreme risk of relying on sudden shifts in trends just to make a couple percentages of returns.

- Basing their trading decisions on hyped information

With today's technology, it is easy to find what the most popular companies are. The news keeps on focusing on these companies. While the news and online publications may seem like they are experts in their fields, very few of them actually know what they are doing. This does not stop those who know nothing about stock investing from discussing the best and worst performers in the market. As a result, we often see hype job companies in the market.

Hyped companies often grow in value. Most of the time, the growth is not sustainable and does not reflect the intrinsic value of the company. Unfortunately, people often fall for these hype jobs because they do not want to be left out of the loop. Instead of investing their money only in their circles of competence, they choose to invest in these hype jobs. This can be dangerous when the investor gets pressured to buy companies he or she knows nothing about.

When investing, stick to your own circle of competence. Also focus on your own legitimate sources of information and avoid publications and media companies that talk about specific stocks. Instead, focus on the raw information you get, like the company's financial reports, as you primary bases for making investing decisions.

Chapter 12 – Important Beginner Tips

"As time goes on, I get more and more convinced that the right method of investment is to put fairly large sums into enterprises which one thinks one knows something about and in the management of which one thoroughly believes."

~J.M. Keynes

As a beginner, you will make mistakes in investing, especially early on. This is inevitable when you are just starting out and you are learning everything on your own. Don't worry if you do make mistakes. Learn from these mistakes and focus more on the actions that you will take in the future.

In this chapter, we will talk about some best practices that you may want to integrate into your investing strategy. Let's begin by creating an investing journal:

Record all your actions

While learning about the stock market, you will often find yourself overwhelmed by all the information in the market. You will need to keep tabs on all your target companies and the companies that you are already invested in. It is understandable to feel overwhelmed.

To keep everything organized, start a journal for your investing activities and thoughts. One way to do this is by putting all your decisions and your reasons behind them in your journal. This will allow you to keep track of all of the strategies that you use. It will allow you to keep track of the strategies that do work.

It also helps to used detailed notes that will allow you to understand why and how you gained or lost money. Aside from your stock picking process, you can also record your basis for choosing one company stock over another. Every time you invest your money, you lose the opportunity to invest in other stocks. It's worth noting why you choose to pick one stock over another. You may include the analytical processes that you chose to use as the basis for your decision.

Make it a habit to read your own journal entries. This is one of the best ways to learn from your own triumphs and mistakes. The investors in the world remember many of their trades. They learn from their past mistakes and, if needed, they adjust their behavior to make sure that these some mistakes are never repeated.

Keep on going even in the face of losses

Losses are inevitable when investing in the stock market. It does not matter if your lose money every now and then. It's impossible to be right all the time. You need to make sure though, that you do not lose more money than you gain. You can do this by making sure that each of your buying decisions is based on sound analysis.

Another way to avoid massive losses is by using the stop loss feature present in most trading software. The stop loss order allows you to set a selling price that tells the broker to sell your position when the price of the stocks you own dips to a certain price line. For instance, you can set a stop loss of 3% below your selling price. If you bought the stocks for $10 each, the stop loss price will be $9.70.

Even if you experience these types of losses, do not feel bad. Let the negative feeling pass and try to learn from your experience. Enter the experience on your journal and try to identify the factors and the decision making process that led to the mistake. A good investor will accept the fact the he or she lost money and move on.

Be wary when everyone is excited

There are times when you will notice that just about every stock in the market seems to be growing in value. All the indices are rising in value and there seems to be a lot of buzz in the stock market. When there is news that the market is booming, you will also see the performance of the stock market reach the primetime news.

These are all signs that there is overbuying in the market. Some overbuying events in the pass just lead to market corrections or a fading of the hype. However, some overbuying events grow so much that it leads into a bubble. An economic bubble happens when the prices of the stock across the board rises way beyond their real or intrinsic value.

There are many reasons for an economic bubble to form. It could be because a certain asset is given too much attention when in reality, it has little to no intrinsic value. This is the case with most of the cryptocurrencies in the market. It was also the case in the Dot Com bubble of the 2000s.

One sign that there is a bubble is the overly aggressive growth of stock prices in the market. The Dow Jones Industrial Average

(DJIA) for instance, grew by approximately 89% from 2002 to the second half of 2007. The growth was followed by the revelation of the massive debt crisis in the housing market which led to the 2008 stock market crash.

Before the crash, everyone was excited about the market. Sales teams used the stock market as their selling point. The excitement, euphoria and the media buzz about the market's performance made more people want to partake. All those who came into the market late lost a big chunk of their investment.

A similar thing happened in the Dot Com bubble in the 2000s. People became excited about the new business concepts brought about by the internet and many of them did not do their due diligence before investing. As a result, many unprofitable business ideas received funding. When all the money was used up with no returns to show for it, things came crashing down.

Before that crash, a similar sequence of events happened. The market boomed. Prices were rising all across the board. There was euphoria among the bulls in the market. At the same time, a lot of unsophisticated investors ended up taking part in the so-called boom. In the end, many people lost more than 40% of their invested amounts. Billions of dollars vanished with all the companies that filed for bankruptcy.

When things are booming in the stock market, you need to be more wary and to avoid getting hooked into the euphoria. Don't get carried away by what the media and the financial experts are telling you. Majority of these experts get it wrong in a crash. If they were right, crashes would have been avoided.

Instead, use stock market booms as a time to exit the market with a profit. One strategy is to start selling off your positions as the big indices start ballooning in value. You could choose to keep your withdrawn money as cash or you could choose to invest them in stable stock alternatives like precious metals.

Avoid Investing with borrowed money

A stock market bubble usually goes on for a few years before it bursts. In the chaos of a bullish market, it is common for people to think that the rise in the stock market will continue. In the process, some people want to maximize the amount of money they earn by using leverage. Leverage in the stock market is just a fancy way of calling loans.

Using loans to invest in the stock market is extremely dangerous. To begin with, borrowed money almost always comes with interest. This interest rate will ultimately be deducted from your profits. It's safe to say that you are starting from a loss when you are investing borrowed money.

It is especially dangerous to use this type of fund if the investments you make do not make money. This happens when you sell your stocks at a loss. Even if you do gain some amount from your losses, you will still lose money if the rate of return does not cover the total interest rate.

When you are investing with borrowed money, you are investing with money that you cannot afford to lose. By doing so, you are significantly increasing the risk of investing. You are risking not only your own money but also your future income. In case you lose all of it, you will end up using your future income to pay all of it back.

Create a Stock Building Circle of Friends

Stock investing is all about monetizing your knowledge about the economy and the companies that are in it. In the previous chapters, we talked about how you could build your circle of influence. This is a list of stock indices and sectors that you are a master of. Over time, you will be better at assessing the situation in these indices and sectors.

Unfortunately, it will be extremely difficult for you to expand that circle of competence on your own. It takes a lot of time to study new companies and when you do start studying companies outside of your circle of competence, you realize how many of these companies turn out to be unprofitable.

This is where the social factor of stock investing comes in. Instead of doing it all on your own, you could enlist your friends who also trade stocks to help you expand your circle of competence. You can choose to create a group that talks about stock investing strategies, picks and other important information.

Each person in the group has his or her own circle of competence. Each week, one person could talk about the companies or industries that they are knowledgeable about. This will help the other members of the team learn about new companies. Each session can have a part where the speaker answers questions about his or her circle of competence. Each member of the group can benefit by listening to what other people has to say about their respective circles of competence.

Learn to hedge your position

At times, there will be a need for you to hedge your position in the stock market. Hedging is a strategy where in you allocate a part of your income to offset the losses that may happen in a high risk stock investment. One example of hedging is putting your money on a competitor of the primary stock you are invested in. If you are invested in a leading car manufacturer for example, you may choose to put part of your funds on its strongest competitor. For instance, you may put your money on the company with the second largest market share.

The best amount to invest when hedging varies, depending on how much you have. A common hedging strategy is to invest 25%-30% of one's fund size into a hedged position.

Another way to do it is by distributing the amount left to the remaining competitors of a big player. If you are invested heavily on General Motors for example, you can choose to invest the rest of your money to multiple other car brands. This will ensure that any losses you may

Don't feel bad for exiting early

The media can be ruthless when judging investors' performances. The investment media often cast a bad light on missing out on profits because of exiting early. Exiting early happens when the price of a particular stock continues to grow after you sold your position.

Many beginner investors feel bad when they miss out on profits after selling off their position. Try not to have the same mindset. Before you make a sale order, list down the reasons why you are selling your position. For instance, you may base your selling decision on fundamental and technical analyses. You may also choose to exit when you have reached your investment goals.

If you exit because of the following reasons and the stock price continues to go up, don't feel bad because your decision fits the best practices of investing. The longer you take to pull your money out, the higher the risk will be of losing, not only your returns, but also a big chunk of your investment.

Another good reason for exiting a position is when you found another investment opportunity to transfer your funds to. If you choose to exit a position in the market for this reason, there is no time to feel bad. Instead of focusing on what might have been, it's better to focus your attention towards your current investments.

Lastly, there are times when we just get it wrong. This happens when our basis for selling our position is based on bad market assumptions. This happens when we use incomplete or inaccurate market information. If this happens, use your investment journal as your outlet for your mistake. Put your mistake into writing to document it and to learn from it.

Conclusion

I hope this book was able to help you to understand the basics of the stock market.

The next important step that you need to take is to start investing and studying the market. Start by studying the market and doing some paper trading in your free time. This will allow you to practice trading without the risk of losing money. It also allows you to test out your preferred investment strategies.

Keep in mind that there is no better training than doing real trades. As soon as you have managed to build your initial capital, you could already start investing on companies that you have full confidence in. Make sure that you are investing at the right time and you know your reasons for entering a position.

With time and experience, you will be able to develop a reliable list of best practices when investing. Stick with these best practices and you will eventually reach your financial goals.

I wish you the best of luck!

To your success,

William Seals

www.ingramcontent.com/pod-product-compliance
Lightning Source LLC
Chambersburg PA
CBHW020447220526
45464CB00002B/890